Ireland

LIBBY KOPONEN

Children's Press®
An Imprint of Scholastic Inc.
New York Toronto London Auckland Sydney
Mexico City New Delhi Hong Kong
Danbury, Connecticut

Content Consultant

Eileen Reilly, D.Phil.
Associate Director, Glucksman Ireland House
New York University
One Washington Mews
New York, NY

Library of Congress Cataloging-in-Publication Data

Koponen, Libby.
 Ireland / by Libby Koponen.
     p. cm. — (A true book)
 Includes bibliographical references and index.

ISBN-13: 978-0-531-16892-9 (lib. bdg.)   978-0-531-21359-9 (pbk.)
ISBN-10: 0-531-16892-1 (lib. bdg.)   0-531-21359-5 (pbk.)

1. Ireland—Juvenile literature. I. Title. II. Series.

 DA906.K67 2009
 941.5—dc22   2008014788

Produced by Weldon Owen Education Inc.

1 2 3 4 5 6 7 8 9 10 R 18 17 16 15 14 13 12 11 10 09

Find the Truth!

Everything you are about to read is true *except* for one of the sentences on this page.

Which one is **TRUE**?

T or F You can find a horse race in Ireland 170 days out of every year.

T or F Ireland is known for its sunny climate.

Find the answers in this book.

Contents

THE **BIG** TRUTH!

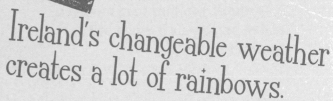

Ireland's changeable weather creates a lot of rainbows.

This Irish sport is Europe's oldest field game.

A lookout tower is built at the highest point of the Cliffs of Moher. It is about 700 feet (213 meters) above sea level. It was built for tourists in 1835.

CHAPTER 1

An Island on the Edge

Ireland is a small island in the Atlantic Ocean, on the western edge of Europe. It is only about the size of South Carolina. Yet its people and culture have made it famous throughout the world. Today, Ireland has two parts. The **Republic** of Ireland is an independent country. A small area called Northern Ireland is a part of the United Kingdom.

No place in Ireland is more than 70 miles (113 kilometers) from the sea.

Immigrants and Invaders

Ireland's first residents arrived about 9,000 years ago. They were probably hunters who **migrated** from Scotland. Over the next thousand years, the population grew. About 400 B.C.E., tribes from mainland Europe, known as Celts (KELTS), invaded. Under the Celts, Irish art and culture flourished. Celtic influence is felt to this day.

The next to invade were warriors from Norway, known as the Vikings. They attacked in the 800s C.E., but eventually retreated.

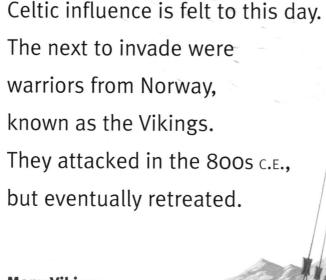

Many Vikings were adventurous sailors. Some of them sailed as far as North America.

Ireland and the United Kingdom

Scotland

Northern Ireland

Belfast

England

Laytown

Irish Sea

Clifden Galway

Republic of Ireland

Dublin

United Kingdom

Atlantic Ocean

Limerick

Cashel

Wales

Killarney

Cork

Celtic Sea

The United Kingdom is made up of England, Scotland, Wales, and Northern Ireland.

In the 1100s, the English invaded the island in large numbers. They stayed for several hundred years. The English owned the best land and held the most important political posts. For some time, it was even illegal to speak Gaelic (GAY-lik), the Irish language. Still, the Irish kept their language and culture alive under foreign rule. Eventually, in the 1900s, the Republic of Ireland was established.

Some parts of Ireland
have more than 220 days
of rain a year.

CHAPTER 2

Green Fields

Ireland is known as The Land of 40 Shades of Green.

Mountains ring the entire island of Ireland, ranging from dramatic cliffs to rounded hills. Grass-covered fields take up most of the central countryside. These fields are so brilliantly green that Ireland is nicknamed "the Emerald Isle."

From Horses to Computers

In much of Ireland, mild winters and rainy weather mean the grass stays green all year. This makes the country perfect for grazing animals such as horses, cattle, and sheep. There are more cattle and sheep than people in the country. Horses are a major Irish industry. People travel from all over the world to buy Irish horses and ponies. Horseback riding and horse racing are popular.

Horse races are held in Ireland on 170 days of the year.

The famous Laytown Races held every year are run on the beach as soon as the tide goes out.

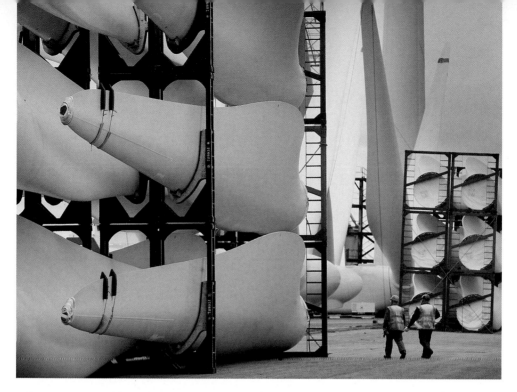

Irish companies supply turbines for many European wind farms. Turbines use giant blades such as these to convert wind energy into electricity.

Industry keeps the Irish economy growing. Ireland's main **export** is computers. International companies that make computers, medicines, and medical devices all have branches in Ireland.

Countryside and Castles

Tourism is another major industry in Ireland. Many visitors are drawn to the beautiful countryside, castles, and ancient sites. Others fish, play golf, ride horses, or enjoy the music in local pubs. Tourists can choose to stay on working farms. Ireland's changeable, often rainy weather doesn't keep tourists away. As the Irish say, "If you don't like the weather, wait five minutes."

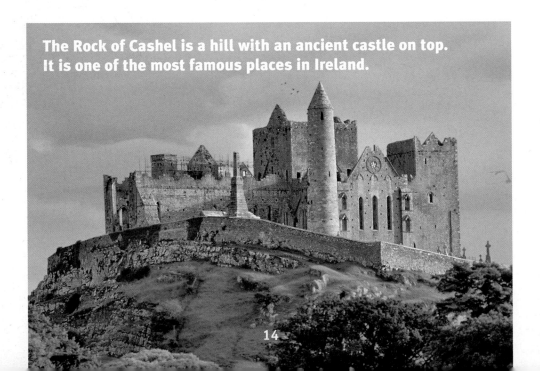

The Rock of Cashel is a hill with an ancient castle on top. It is one of the most famous places in Ireland.

Spire of Light

The Dublin Spire is the tallest structure in the city of Dublin. It stands 394 feet (120 meters) tall. The elegant monument was built in 2003 to replace a monument called Nelson's Pillar, which was destroyed by a bomb in 1966. The design was chosen in an international contest. Depending on the time of day, the stainless steel surface can appear to be different colors.

In bright sunlight the Dublin Spire can be seen for miles around.

Newgrange Tomb was built in about 3200 B.C.E. The tomb was designed so that the December sun lights up the whole inner burial chamber, that has walls lined with gold.

CHAPTER 3

Warriors and Scholars

The Irish people have had a dramatic history. They have experienced war and invasions. They have also had a time so glorious that it is called the Golden Age. Millions died or left the country during a terrible **famine**. This changed the country's history. Yet Ireland survived and is now stronger than ever before.

Newgrange Tomb is about 500 years older than the Great Pyramid of Egypt.

The Celts in Ireland

After the Celts invaded Ireland, many settled there. The Celts valued learning and the arts, especially writing and music. Their storytellers, called bards, were among the most respected people in the community. Celtic craftspeople were also skilled at making jewelry and ornaments.

The Celts divided Ireland into small territories. The tribal rulers of these territories often fought with each other. However, they all agreed on the authority of the Druids. The Druids were learned teachers and priests who believed in gods of nature. Druids made laws and settled disputes.

People believed that Druids could predict the future. Tribal rulers came to them for advice.

Celtic Laws

Celtic tribal territories were united by language, culture, and a system of laws. These laws were highly detailed and often very fair. For example, women could own property, which was unusual at that time. Thieves were punished more severely for stealing from the poor than from the rich. Celtic laws and customs lasted in Ireland for more than 1,000 years.

The Irish have used the Celtic high cross for centuries. Some of these crosses can still be seen on church grounds today.

The Golden Age

Legend has it that about 400 C.E., a young man from England named Patrick chased the snakes out of Ireland. This probably meant that he drove out the Druids. Patrick, who later became Saint Patrick, spread Christianity throughout the land.

From about 500 C.E., most of Europe was at war, following the breakup of the Roman Empire. But in Ireland, poets, intellectuals, and musicians continued to flourish. This period of more than 300 years is often called the Golden Age of Ireland.

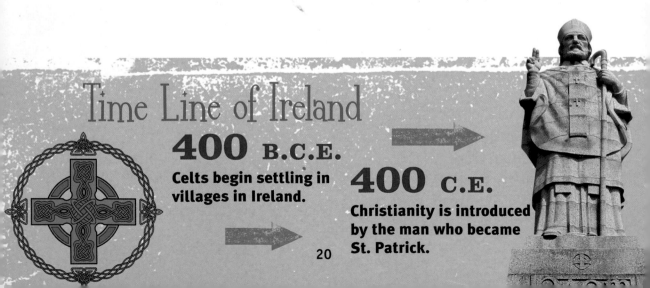

Time Line of Ireland

400 B.C.E.
Celts begin settling in villages in Ireland.

400 C.E.
Christianity is introduced by the man who became St. Patrick.

English Control

Ireland's Golden Age slowly came to an end in the 800s. This is when the Vikings started to raid **monasteries** and villages. Ireland held its own until 1169, when the English invaded. For the next 750 years, England controlled much of Irish life. In later years they favored the Irish Protestants and often treated Roman Catholics badly. Thousands of Irish Catholics were sent to the Americas in the 1600s. Later, Catholics were not allowed to own land or speak Gaelic. English landlords owned all property and rented only small plots to the Irish to farm.

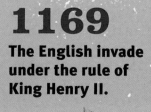

1169

The English invade under the rule of King Henry II.

1922

The Irish Free State, now the Republic of Ireland, is formed.

Children helped their families dig the earth in hope of finding food.

Years of Hunger

Irish **tenant farmers** depended on a single crop, the potato, to feed their families. Other farm products were collected by landlords and sent to England. Then, in 1845, the Irish potato crop failed for several years. The peasants had no food and no income. Many were thrown out of their homes as they could not pay rent. They wandered the countryside dying of hunger and sickness. Whole villages were wiped out. Millions sailed to America and more than a million died.

The Troubles

By the late 1800s, the Irish wanted more of a say in governing the country. However, there was conflict between Catholics and the Protestant **minority**. In 1922, after years of fighting, the largely Catholic Republic of Ireland was formed in the south.

In Northern Ireland, the Catholic minority felt they had fewer rights than Protestants. They wanted a **unified** Irish Republic. A violent struggle broke out in the 1960s. This period, known as the Troubles, did not end until 2003. The island is now at peace but remains divided.

Peace walls remain in Belfast, in Northern Ireland. They separate Catholic and Protestant neighborhoods to avoid conflict.

Peace wall

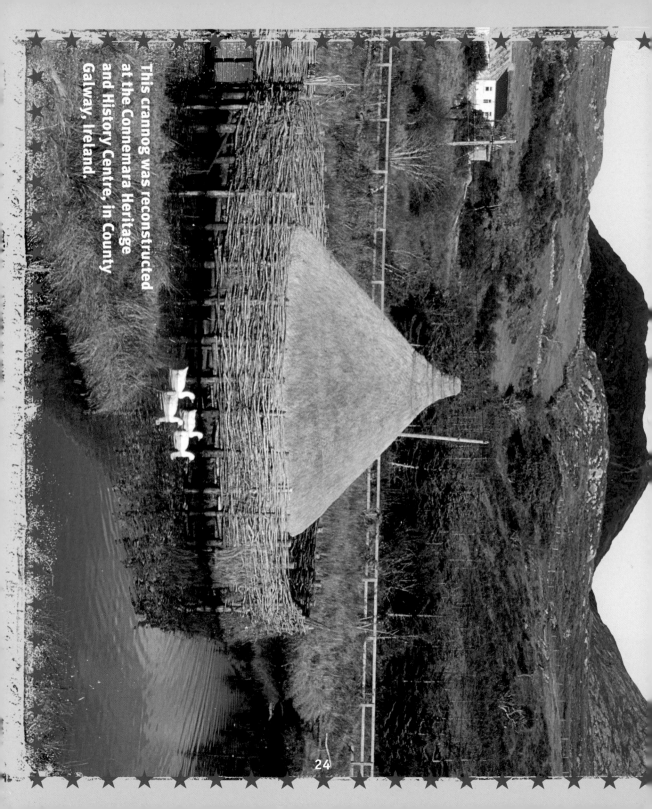

This crannog was reconstructed at the Connemara Heritage and History Centre, in County Galway, Ireland.

Fairy Forts

Crannogs were fortified dwellings built on artificial islands in lakes. They were round and up to 200 ft (60 m) across. Historians think that most crannogs were built after the arrival of the Celts in 400 B.C.E. The Celts brought iron tools and weapons. They also fought frequently among themselves.

Making a Crannog

Crannog builders began by driving a framework of poles into the lakebed. They filled this with earth, rocks, logs, and branches. Once the foundation was above water level, they made the crannog itself from wood. The word *crannog* comes from "tree" in Old Irish.

The End of the Crannog

Crannogs could withstand bows and arrows, but not cannons! From about the 1500s, most crannogs were abandoned and eventually crumbled. But some crannogs survive to this day throughout Ireland. The Irish call the mounds left over from the crannogs "fairy forts."

25

The Corrs are a famous Irish pop band. They play traditional instruments such as the penny whistle and fiddle.

26

CHAPTER 4

Treasures

Ireland is the only country in the world with a musical instrument (the harp) for its national emblem.

Since the days of the Celts, Ireland has shown a love for beauty and art. Today, the Irish are still known for their creativity in literature, music, dance, painting, and other forms of art. There are many museums and art galleries across the country. Much of the current art builds on the nation's rich traditions.

Beautiful Books

In **medieval** times, Irish monks created **illuminated** books to spread Christian teachings. One visitor said these beautiful books looked as if angels had made them. The books showed scenes from daily life. The monks used brilliantly colored inks to decorate their manuscripts. Some of the inks were made from native plants. Some were brought to Ireland at great cost. Sometimes the monks added gold for an even richer effect.

The man who became Saint Columba may have written parts of a famous manuscript, the *Book of Kells*.

Jonathan Swift was an Irish writer. His most famous book was *Gulliver's Travels*.

Gulliver is captured by people who are 6 inches (15 centimeters) tall.

Timeless Tales

Ever since the bards spun tales during the Golden Age, the Irish have told stories. The main characters were often imaginary creatures such as ghosts, giants, or leprechauns. In recent times, four Irish authors have won the famous Nobel Prize in Literature. Today, the Irish government helps to continue the tradition by supporting authors. Ireland is the only country in the world where writers don't have to pay taxes.

Song and Dance

Music has long been an important part of Irish life. Paid musicians are not the only ones who play traditional Irish music. When musicians perform in country pubs today, people bring their own instruments and join in. They may play fiddle, pipes, penny whistles, or drums. If someone in the village is known to have a good voice, the audience will ask that person to sing a song.

Traditional Irish music is kept alive by people of all ages. The Irish drum is called a bodhran (BOW-rahn).

Irish dancing is popular with people of all ages. Many children study step dancing in school. At the All-Celtic Festival, people dance in a traditional style called *sean-nós*. There aren't any fixed steps. Traditionally, these rhythmic dances were performed on a wooden door laid on ground. This is why *sean-nós* performers stay on one spot as they dance.

Step dancing costumes are based on Irish peasant dress. Most are decorated with hand-sewn Celtic designs.

Castles and Cottages

Although Ireland has castles and beautiful large stone country houses, these were mainly built for the English. Until as recently as 50 years ago, most Irish people lived in cottages. These were made of whitewashed local stone. They had thick walls and small windows to keep in the heat. Wooden beams held up the thatched or slate roofs. The clay floors were often damp and sometimes turned to mud. Many had only one or two rooms.

In some places in Ireland, it is illegal to tear down old cottages. People often fix them up and use them as vacation homes.

The Celtic knot pattern is found on many ancient ornaments such as this one.

This pattern has become popular again with modern Irish artists and jewelry designers.

Irish Patterns

Celtic art features intricate patterns made mostly of curving lines. Spirals and knots are common design elements. Sometimes animals and people are hidden in the patterns.

Traditional patterns are also used to knit what are known as fisherman's sweaters. The Aran Islands are off Ireland's western coast. Fishermen's families there still knit using patterns their families invented hundreds of years ago. Today, these sweaters are sold around the world.

Many signposts in the Republic of Ireland are written in Gaelic with the English place-names below.

CHAPTER 5

Still Irish

Most people in Ireland today live near cities. Their lives are similar in many ways to our own. But daily life in Ireland has some surprising differences. Much of the difference has to do with the land itself and with traditions that have not died out.

Gaelic is still spoken and read in some parts of Ireland.

Day by Day

One particular Irish practice is the use of **peat** as fuel. Peat is found in bogs in many parts of Ireland. A bog is an area of wet, spongy land. Here, peat forms from rotted plant remains. It is dug out, then cut into slabs and dried. Dried peat can be burned in fireplaces. The scent of a peat fire is a comforting relief from Ireland's cool, damp climate. Some Irish power plants get energy from burning peat as well.

Peat can be shaped into small blocks called briquettes. These can be stacked easily like firewood.

Peat briquettes

Irish Schools

School in Ireland is different, too. Gym class includes dance, outdoor adventure, and water sports. All students learn Gaelic, also called Irish.

Ireland has one of the best educational systems in the world. Students must attend school until at least the age of 15. College is free. Almost everyone in Ireland can read and write.

Students at most Irish schools wear uniforms.

Fast Sports

Traditional sports and dances are as much a part of life for Ireland's young people as are television and computers. Horseback riding has always been a popular sport. But Gaelic football and hurling, played by both boys and girls, are beloved for being uniquely Irish.

Hurling is a fast-moving ball game that is popular with Irish people of all ages. Some version of the game has been played in Ireland since ancient times. It is similar to both lacrosse and field hockey. Hurling uses an ax-shaped stick, or hurley, to get a small ball across a goal.

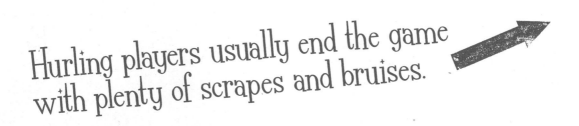

Hurling players usually end the game with plenty of scrapes and bruises.

Hurling used to be a game played by neighboring communities. There was no limit to the number of players on each side.

Gaelic Football

Gaelic football may well have come from an ancient Celtic game. It was already popular in the 1500s and is still played today. It's similar to soccer and rugby. However, it is Ireland's own game and a source of great national pride. The play is rough-and-tumble, exciting, and risky. Players wear little protective gear.

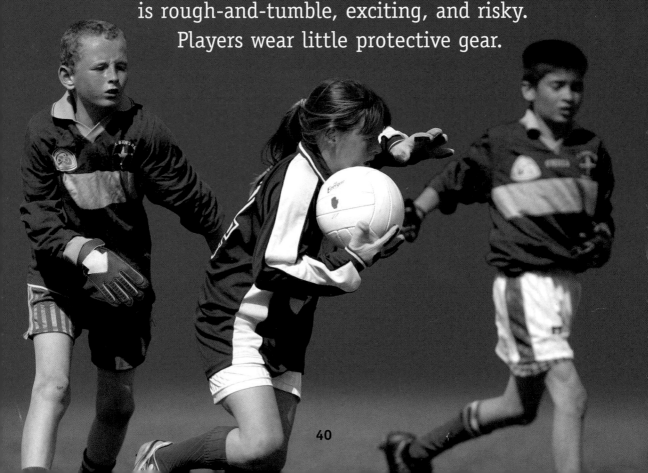

Churchgoers

Religion played an important role in Ireland's history. Today, the majority of the population is Christian. Many people go to church regularly. Most people in the Republic of Ireland are Catholics. In Northern Ireland, Protestants outnumber Catholics slightly.

In both the north and south, Saint Patrick's Day, Good Friday, and Easter Monday are national holidays.

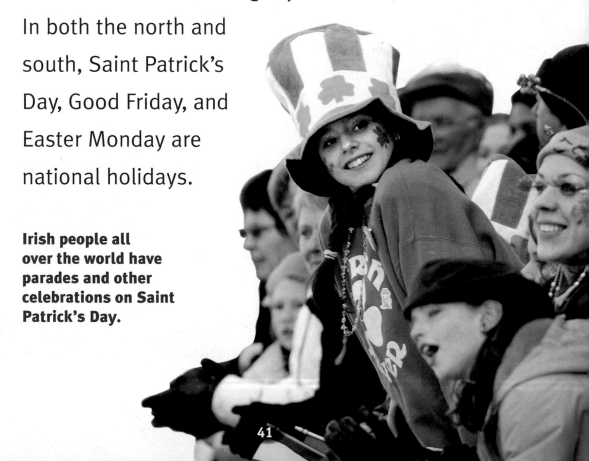

Irish people all over the world have parades and other celebrations on Saint Patrick's Day.

Ireland is now the second-richest country in Europe. This is remarkable because Ireland is small and has few natural **resources**. Being English-speaking is an advantage to Ireland in the business world. The high level of education also helps. The Irish government welcomes foreign companies, as well. All of this may help Ireland continue to prosper in the future. ★

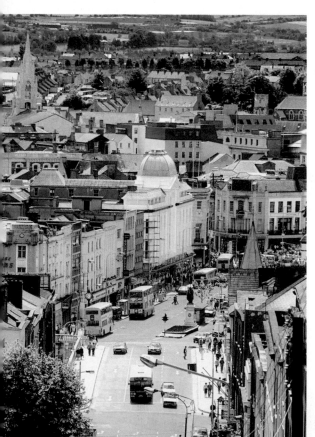

The city of Cork is in the far south of the island. It is the second largest city in the Republic of Ireland.

In 2005, Cork was named a European City of Culture.

True Statistics

THE REPUBLIC OF IRELAND

Counties: 26

Population: About 4,160,000

Longest River: The River Shannon 240 mi. (386 km.)

National Symbol: The harp

Length of coastline: 900 mi. (1448 km.)

Currency: Euro

Literacy rate of those over 15: 99 percent

NORTHERN IRELAND

Counties: 6

Population: About 1,740,000

Border with Republic: 223 mi. (359 km.)

Currency: Pound sterling

Did you find the truth?

(T) You can find a horse race in Ireland 170 days out of every year.

(F) Ireland is known for its sunny climate.

Resources

Books

Blashfield, Jean. *Ireland* (Enchantment of the World). New York: Children's Press, 2002.

Bowden, Rob, and Ronan Foley. *Focus on Ireland*. Milwaukee, WI: World Almanac Library, 2008.

Gottfried, Ted. *Northern Ireland: Peace in Our Time?* Brookfield, CT: Millbrook Press, 2002.

Lyons, Mary. *Feed the Children First: Irish Memories of the Great Hunger*. New York: Atheneum Books for Young Readers, 2002.

McQuinn, Anna. *Ireland* (Countries of the World). Washington, DC: National Geographic, 2008.

Simpson, Margaret. *The Top Ten Irish Legends*. New York: Scholastic Inc., 2000.

Time-Life Books. *What Life Was Like Among Druids and High Kings: Celtic Ireland AD 400–1200*. Alexandria, VA: Time-Life, 1998.

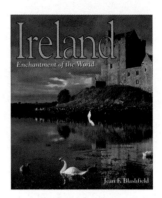

Organizations and Web Sites

Granuaile—Sea Queen of Ireland

www.graceomalley.com
Learn about the real pirate queen, Grace O'Malley
(Granuaile in Gaelic).

St Patrick's National School

www.whitechurchns.ie/Welcome%20Page.htm
Read what Irish schoolchildren in grades 3–6 have to say
about their school.

Travel for Kids

www.travelforkids.com/Funtodo/Ireland/ireland.htm
Find out about great things for children to do on a visit to
Ireland.

Places to Visit

Irish Hunger Memorial

290 Vesey Street and North
End Avenue
New York, NY
Here you will find a half-acre
(0.9-hectare) park filled with
Irish grasses and flowers from
Ireland.

Newgrange Tomb

Brú na Bóinne Visitor Centre
Donore, Co. Meath, Ireland
+353 (41) 988 0300
See the oldest solar
observatory in the world. You
can also visit a 335-acre
(136-ha) working farm nearby.

Important Words

export – goods sent to another country to be sold there

famine (FAM-uhn) – an extreme shortage of food

illuminate (i-LOO-muh-nate) – to decorate a text with gold, silver, or other brillant colors, elaborate designs, and pictures

medieval (med-ee-EE-vuhl) – referring to the Middle Ages period of history between about 500 C.E. and 1450 C.E.

migrate – to move from one place or country to another

minority – a population group that is smaller in number than other groups in an area

monastery – a place where monks live and work

peat – marshy soil that is made up of decomposed plants

republic – a country controlled by a government and its president, not a king or queen

resource – a stock or supply of materials

tenant farmer – a farmer who rents a property that belongs to someone else

unify – to bring or join together into a whole or unit

Index

Page numbers in **bold** indicate illustrations

About the Author

Libby Koponen is the author of other True Books and *Blow Out the Moon*, a novel based on a true story about an American girl who goes to an English boarding school. Libby has a B.A. in history from Wheaton College and an M.F.A. from Brown University in writing. She has traveled all over the world and ridden horses in every continent except Antarctica. She has been to Ireland several times and visited many of the places in this book.

PHOTOGRAPHS © 2009: Big Stock Photo (©David Kerr, p. 6; ©Le Do, p. 43; ©Stephen Jones, Saint Patrick, p. 20;); Dreamstime.com (©Aleksey Shkipin, cross, p. 20); Getty Images (pp. 12–13; King Henry II, p. 21); iStockphoto.com (©Andrew Bardsley, p. 32; ©Manuela Weschke, p. 19; ©Marco Testa, p. 10; ©Nathan Gleave, p. 36; ©Paul Cowan, flag, p. 21; ©Ramon Rodriguez, rainbow, p. 5; Robert Simon, p. 3; ©Sarah Bossert, back cover); Photolibrary (front cover; p. 15; p. 18; p. 23; p. 28; p. 42); photonewzealand/alamy (p. 30; pp. 34–35; pp. 39–40); Tranz (Corbis, p. 14; p. 16; p. 22; p. 24; p. 29; p. 31; p. 33; p. 37; p. 41; Rex Features, p. 26)